I'm So Happy

Marvin Heiferman

and

Carole Kismaric

VINTAGE BOOKS · A DIVISION OF RANDOM HOUSE, INC. · NEW YORK

No man is happy

except by comparison.

In spontaneous smiles, the cheeks
move up and the muscles tighten,
making crow's feet. And if the real
smile is large enough, the skin
around the eyebrow droops down a

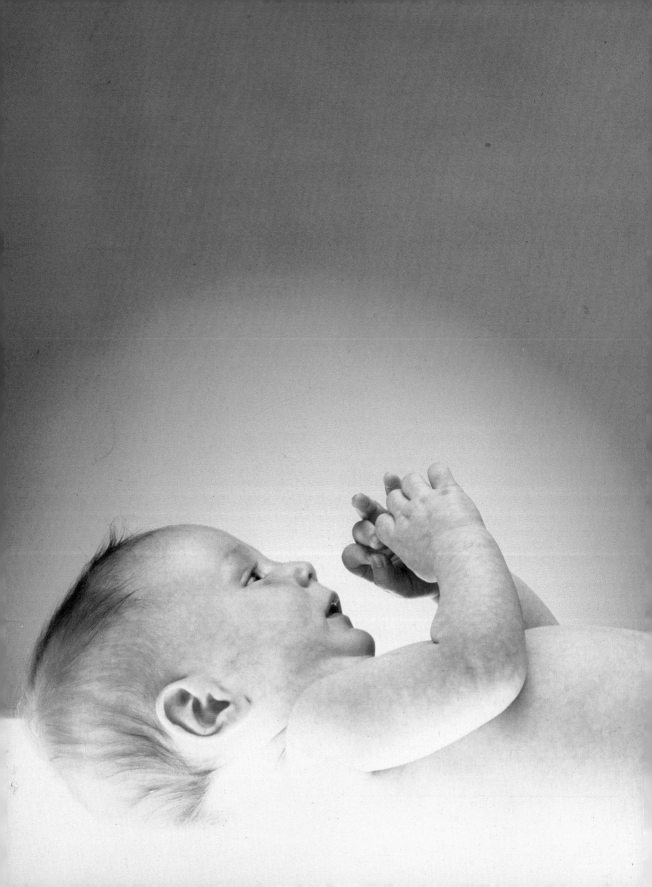

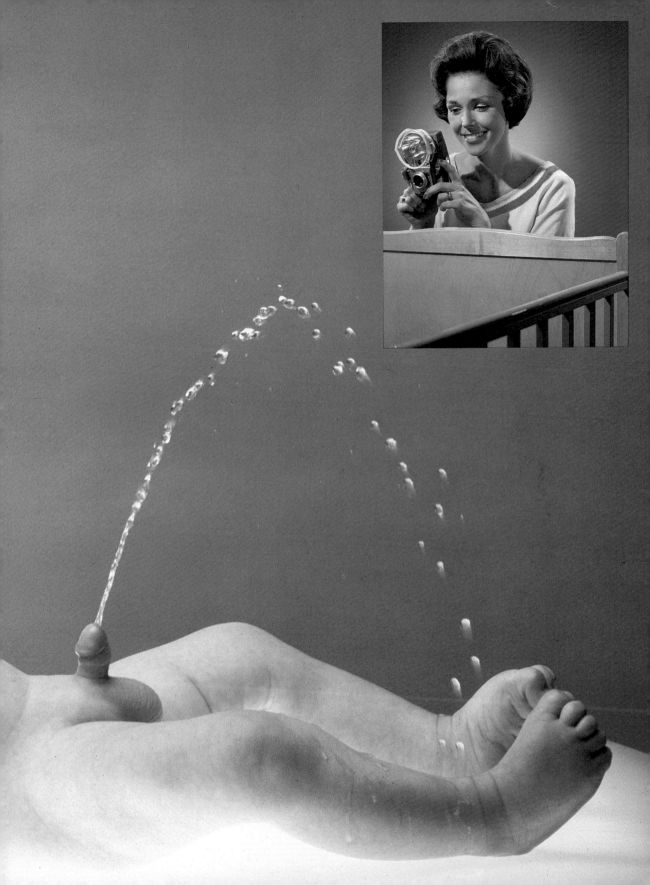

What is happiness? The feeling that power increases, that resistance is overcome.

There are no happy lives, only happy moments.

In a genuine, happy smile, the muscle around the eye, called the orbicularis oculi, tightens while another muscle, zygomatic major, pulls the lip corners upward.

Dinah Shore "Be Bop a Lula" cooking Spaghetti O's Toni permanents snowed-in first day of school Bosco Debbie weds Curious George the wind ice cream man snap, crackle, pop Flash Gordon Ding Dong School Florida state rock 'n' roll Winkletter Pez training wheels snores Cinderella Paradise fluoride toothpaste World drive-up bank window shorts Park back seat listens dry beds Lik-em-Aid clean Yogi Michael Jackson Froggie the Gremlin Willie Mays lunchbox happy school colored Mr. Clean getting invited to a party Pick-Up-Sticks cha-cha-cha Betty Crocker Heckel and Jeckel "Hey kids. What time is it?" throwing a ball skating in the basement plastic glasses teacher's pet painting by numbers Jimmy Durante Chatty Cathy power mowers The Adventures of Superman music lessons Arthur Murray first library card reading comic books Imogene Coca Sluggo and Nancy and Aunt Fritzi blowing up the swimming pool Cowboys and Indians Edsel getting mail eating bologna "Does She or Doesn't She?" Creamsicles Lincoln Logs dolls that walk The Family of Man Confidential two-tone cars cleaning erasers catching fireflies making pudding Treasure Hunt June Taylor dancers "Filter, Flavor, Flip-top Box" Dinah Shore "Be Bop a Lula" cooking Spaghetti O's Toni permanents snowed-in first day of

Even laughing and smiling require time and practice before the ability to do so is fully developed. Although Darwin observed the first smile by the seventh or eighth week of a child's life, he was unable to distinguish clearly incipient laughter in his children until some eight or nine weeks later.

Some people spread happiness wherever they go, others whenever they go.

The supreme happiness of life is the conviction that we are loved.

Khrushchev goes to Disneyland Ayn Rand miniature golf piggy sales exceed $1 billion Sweet Home Oregon Mickey Mantle Mr. Potato Head *The Cat in the Hat* bare feet *Junior Scholastic* *The Little Engine That Could* God toys instant coffee Liberace Viewmaster *Davy Crockett* Kool-Aid Ernie Kovacs Boeing 707 flies "Wake Up, *I Love Lucy* Hank Aaron Candid Camera Boogaloo Ralph Kramden Little Richard Little Rickie Cheerios washer-dryer introduced pageboys Etch A Sketch The Jerk Jack Lemmon *The Price Is Right Lassie* hobbies Sputnik launched "Great Balls of Fire" Fab Wham-O Frisbee Saturday TV playing outside late "What me worry?" summer camp reading Nancy D Stroll Ole ning a Gigi sold cle Eater slee at a fri a pen pal restaura twirling a *The Little R one Alaska becomes a state s ncyclopedia ice cream sandwic the last day of school front-row movie seats All Shook Up starching crinolines stepping on a crack stamp collecting Girl Scout cookies *77 Sunset Strip* Velveeta cheese *Profiles in Courage* Visible Man mayonnaise sandwiches Visible Woman *Dragnet The Chipmunks West Side Story* Coco Marsh Mallomars *The Jetsons* Bonomo Turkish Taffy Kim Novak *Car 54, Where Are You?* fluoridated water fireworks *Candid Camera* first day of school going bowling school trips Cheez-Wiz camp counselors Khrushchev goes to Disneyland Ayn Rand miniature golf piggy bank

Happiness is like jam; you can't spread it without getting some on yourself.

Those who release more endorphins may be happier about any given situation in their lives that those with fewer endorphins.

Happiness, then, is real and has a molecular basis

To be without some of the things you want is an indispensable part of happiness.

Queen for a Day   buying 45s   training bras   The Stroll   Classic Comics   Mary Poppins   teacher's pet   Looney Toons   "works and plays well with others"   Liz Taylor marries   The Flintstones   The Twist   Ricky Nelson   no homework   The Hand Jive   My Fair Lady   Friend   Nebraska   Almond Joy   "Personality"   Jerry Lewis   "Yakety Yak"   getting an autograph   Ambush   Barbie dolls   The Donna Reed Show   polio vaccine   The Walk   Lady Chatterley's Lover   "Love Potion Number 9"   Chanukah   knowing the answer   double features   Merryville Louisiana   Topper   calypso   getting an allowance   savings account interest rises to 4 percent   "Itsy Bitsy Teenie Weenie Yellow Polka Dot Bikini"   movie stars   tutti-frutti   punching a friend   Annette   passing a note   "Doo Wah Diddy"   Goldfinger   Seventeen   Where the Boys Are   Mad   Candy   zip codes   suntan lotion   valentines   La Dolce Vita   personal disposable income $352   chinos   Hayley Mills   "I Have a Dream"   Ken dolls   Cliffs Notes   Pleasantville Ohio   potato chips   buying your own pizza   "At the Hop"   making the team   Astroturf   The Beach Boys   clear skin   Bullwinkle Fresca   The Many Loves of Dobie Gillis   going on an airplane   drawers   Route 66   stealing money   "I Like It Like That"   Future Teacher   "Monster Mash"   staying home alone Daniel   band   Camelot   The Sea of Tranquility band   Chinese food   The Patty Duke Show sleep   ice skating   Yogi Berra Lolita   Bachelor Father   Queen for a Day   The Stroll   Classic Comics Mary   Looney Toons   "works and plays   lor marries   The Flintstones The   homework   The Hand Jive My   Almond Joy   "Personality" Jerry   ing an autograph   Ambush

Happy people are always more likely to see the glass as half full rather than half empty.

The action that produces the greatest happiness for the greatest numbers is best.

isn't your position that makes you happy or unhappy, it's your disposition.

"most likely to succeed" "Let the Good Times Roll" cool clothes "You're the squarest" making up your own rules "Things Go Better with Coke" G.I. Joe *The Sound of Music* *Peyton Place* a handsome president tail fins *American Bandstand* hanging out talking on the telephone *April Love* Bermuda shorts Esalen Institute electric knives *A Catcher in the Rye* The Purple People Eater" Elvis "Venus" Fresca mops The Supremes Andy motorcycles hot dogs Gidget Corps roller skating Bobby Heaven Johnny Mathis Liz Taylor kes Sunshine Alaska *Dr. Zhivago* Tang Valium The Locomotion .7 years *Calories Don't Count* bouffant hair man walks in space sneaking a cigarette juke boxes white sneakers tube tops team jackets gossip having a boyfriend shoplifting having a girlfriend buying your own clothes getting a learner's permit candystripers remembering your combination *Marjorie Morningstar* passing a test cheating drive-ins loud music starvation diets The Bristol Stomp "My Boyfriend's Back" air conditioners The Shangri-La's *Meet the Beatles* onion dip hydrogen peroxide *My Favorite Martian* ponytails "most likely to succeed" "Let the Good Times Roll" cool clothes smoking nonfilter cigarettes tufted is best. Dave Brubeck "You're the squarest" making up your own rules "Things Go Better with Coke" G.I. Joe *The Sound of Music* *Peyton Place* a handsome president tail fins *American Bandstand* hanging out talking on the telephone *April Love* Bermuda shorts Esalen Institute electric knives *A Catcher in the Rye* The New Frontier Purple People Eater" Elvis "Venus" Fresca Connie Stevens

TRIPLE LETTER SCORE

TRIPLE LETTER SCORE

DOUBLE WORD SCORE

F_4

DOUBLE LETTER SCORE

DOUBLE LETTER SCORE

DOUBLE WORD SCORE

H_4 O_1 M_3 E_1

DOUBLE WORD SCORE

DOUBLE WORD SCORE

DOUBLE WORD SCORE

O_1 D_2

DOUBLE WORD SCORE

D_2

TRIPLE LETTER SCORE

TRIPLE LETTER SCORE

U_1

DOUBLE LETTER SCORE

C_3 L_1 O_1 T_1 H_4 E_1 S_1

T_1

A_1

DOUBLE LETTER SCORE

W_4 A_1 C_3 A_1 T_1 I_1 O_1 N_1

DOUBLE LETTER SCORE

A_1 I_1

TRIPLE LETTER SCORE

TRIPLE LETTER SCORE

DOUBLE WORD SCORE

R_1 O_1

DOUBLE WORD SCORE

DOUBLE WORD SCORE

N_1

DOUBLE WORD SCORE

DOUBLE LETTER SCORE

DOUBLE LETTER SCORE

DOUBLE WORD SCORE

TRIPLE LETTER SCORE

TRIPLE LETTER SCORE

DOUBLE WORD SCORE

If ignorance is bliss, then why isn't the world happier?

People are happier and kinder on days when the sun is shining and the humidity is low. These effects probably reflect some primitive response to the environment. On sunny days more people stop to help with sociological studies, and they tip waitresses more

It was found that if an electrode was inserted in the pleasure center of the rat's brain, electrical impulses were so rewarding that the animal would press a bar as many as 10,000 times per hour for up to twenty-six hours.

A lifetime of happiness! No man alive could bear it; it would be hell on earth

Each time the face is stretched in an excess smile, some collagen sheets break forever; keratin coils crumple and never properly refold. Combined with the drying and loosening all aging skin has to go through, that adds up.

**You'll be happy
if you stop worrying
because
you're not.**

27,000,000 blenders sold   going to weddings   Opportunity
Montana   singles bars   *M*A*S*H*   Elton John   double-knit
suits   public TV   getting a raise   blind dates   Stevie Wonder
death penalty declared unconstitutional   *Let's Make a Deal*   Bob
and Carol and Ted and Alice   volleyball   *People*   Cuisinart   bub-
ble gum rock   lunching with the boss   Germaine Greer   Farrah
shopping on   ...   lowered to 18
All in the Fam...   "Nights
in White Sat...   going home for
Christmas   ...   Mississippi
O. J. Simpso...   erner Erhart
Linda Ronst...   income $695
Bliss Nevada...   antz   Monty
Python   plat...   ee gum   the
Bicentennia...   nstitutional
the dry look...   speaks   the
layered look   compact cars   John Belushi   having an answering
machine   Antonioni   wearing white patent leather belts   Gianni
Versace   renting a time share   Tylenol   sipping a Heineken
polyester   "Love Train"   string art   the Bee Gees   RV's   Green-
peace   bumper stickers   almond colored appliances   Handi-
Wipes   no-fault insurance   oversize peppermills   Catherine
Deneuve   Cabbage Patch dolls   child-proof packaging   chocolate-
chip-cookie franchises   *The Best and the Brightest*   sprayed
ceilings   MDA   invisible braces   Peter Bogdanovich   paralegals
hair weaving   lead-free gas   "Midnight at the Oasis"   The
Agnews   the Canadian Film Board   Wash 'n' Dries   free-
basing   Velcro sneaker closings   blush-on   Countess Mara   after-
dinner drinks   Brooke Shields   low-tar cigarettes   the Whalers
wide ties   low-cholesterol nachos   Weight Watchers   the Jackson
Five   double-knit   the Scarsdale Diet   *Last Tango in Paris*
27,000,000 blenders sold   going to weddings   Opportunity

Happiness is courage and work, energy and, above all, illusion.

Manics wear smart, loud clothes and are very pleased with themselves, are smiling, alert, and have a loud, confident voice. They enjoy making speeches and writing letters to important people. This often leads to a successful career in one of the more colorful occupations, such as politics and show business.

One feels inclined to say that the intention that man should be "happy" is not included in the plan of "Creation." What we call happiness comes from the satisfaction of needs that have been dammed up to a great extent, and it is by its very nature only possible as an episodic phenomenon.... We are so made that we can derive intense enjoyment only from a contrast and very little from a constant state of things.

For happy people, time tends to be organized and planned; they are punctual and efficient.

Insincere smiling calls out unwanted platelets. Over seven miles of tiny blood vessels are contorted and compressed when you hold a smile for a five-minute stroll—the length of a crowded cocktail party or business social.

satellite dishes   visiting a theme park   white wine   using over-
draft privileges   microchips   seatbelts are law   Laura Ashley
Nautilus machines   oil prices drop   the wet look   Pee-wee
Herman   Oprah   investing in tax shelters   pocket-sized TVs
thirtysomething   Armani   Roy Cohn dies   potpourri   David
Letterman   Shirley MacLaine born again   *Monday Night Football*   Godiva chocolates   diet colas   two-income families   Häagen
Dazs   800 numbers   buying a Saab   pouf dresses   Reeboks
Jesse Jackson   Palladium   take-out food   *She's Gotta Have It*
people of color   Jim and Tammy Faye   *Mork and Mindy*   low-salt
foods   surrogate mothers   Leona Helmsley   hospices   take-over
artists   freezing pesto   using Combat   sashimi   Don and Melanie
marry again   the Sears Tower   telephone sex   buyer protection
plans   Donal...   ...nks   *Endless*
Love   car ste...   ...eo-Classicism
The Silver Pa...   ...s   liposuction
Beaujolais N...   ...a theme park
white wine   u...   ...seatbelts are
law   Laura A...   ...drop   the wet
look   Pee-wee...   ...elters   pocket-
sized TVs   *th...*   ...ies   potpourri
David Letterm...   ...*Monday Night*
Football   Goo...   ...come families
Häagen Daz...   ...pouf dresses
Reeboks   Jes...   ...d   *She's Gotta*
Have It   peop...   ...*ork and Mindy*
low-salt foods...   ...sley   hospices
take-over arti...   ...sashimi   Don
and Melanie r...   ...one sex   buyer
protection p...   ...*land*   sperm
...anks   *Endless Love*   car stereo systems   grilled arugola   Neo-
Classicism   The Silver Palette   gold cards   friendly take-overs

Happiness is a way station between too much and too little.

JARMAN

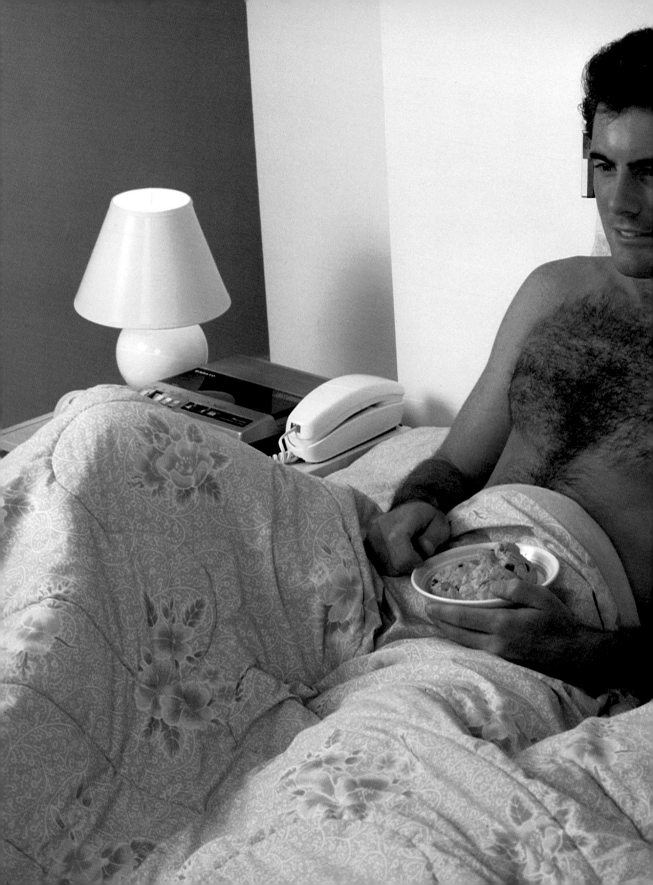

Grimacing leaves its mark, at least for those over forty. It's been estimated that 200,000 frowns will produce one permanent wrinkle.

Most people are about as happy as they make up their minds to be.

It may be said that every individual man and all men in common aim at a certain end. This end, to sum it up briefly, is happiness and its constituents….Let us, then, by way of illustration only, ascertain what is in general the nature of happiness, and what are the elements of its constituent parts. For all advice to do things or not to do them is concerned with happiness and with the things that make for or against it; whatever destroys or hampers happiness, or gives rise to its opposite, we ought not to do.

We may define happiness as prosperity combined with excellence; or as independence of life; or as the secure enjoyment of the maximum of pleasure; or as a good condition of property and body, together with the power of guarding one's property and body and making use of them. That happiness is one or more of these things, pretty well everybody agrees.

From this definition of happiness it follows that its constituent parts are: good birth, plenty of friends, good friends, wealth, good children, plenty of children, a happy old age, also such bodily excellences as health, beauty, strength, large stature, athletic powers, together with fame, honor, good luck, and excellence. A man cannot fail to be completely independent if he possesses these internal and these external goods; for besides these there are no others to have. Goods of the soul and of the body are internal. Good birth, friends, money, and honor are external. Further, we think that he should possess resources and luck in order to make his life really secure.

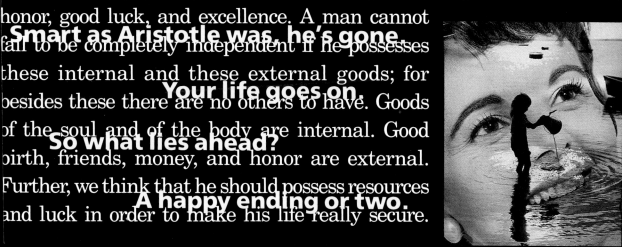

Smart as Aristotle was, he's gone.

Your life goes on.

So what lies ahead?

A happy ending or two.

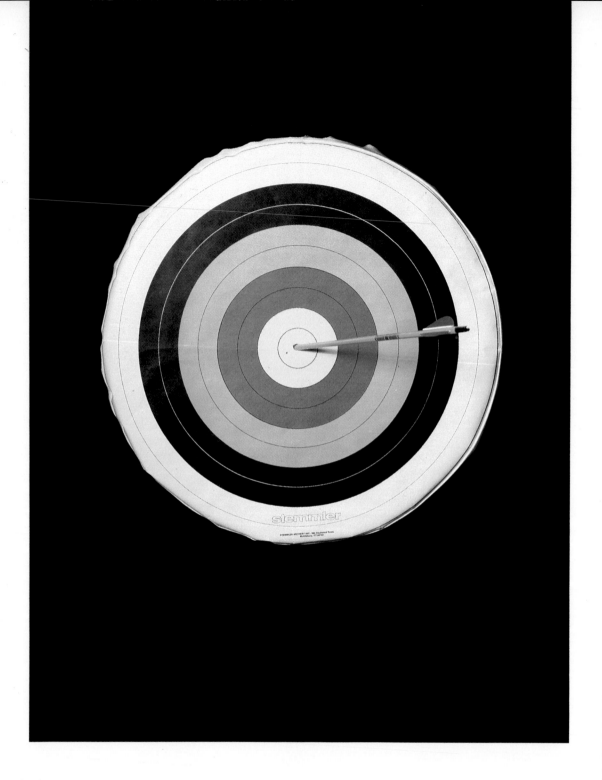

You got it! The promotion, the raise, the partnership. You win the
lottery. Big bucks. Money. Success. You invest. You reinvest. More.

The kids grow up. They're well adjusted, drug-free. They leave home and you're free. And they call every week, like clockwork. Perfect.

Your house triples in value, and the neighborhood is crime-free.
Cities stay solvent. Taxes go down. You buy that second home. Relax

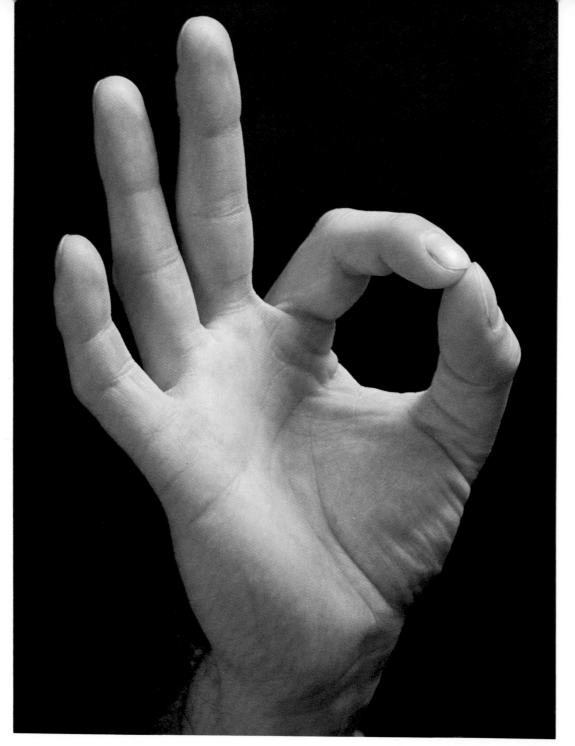

It's 2040, late in the evening, and you're having a glass of warm milk. The TV is on, you put down your favorite book, rest your head on the pillow, and fall comfortably into a very deep sleep with a smile on your face. Peace.

ACKNOWLEDGMENTS

Thanks to Mary Shanahan and Adam Gopkik for getting *I'm So Happy* off the ground. Gwen Darien of the Institute for Contemporary Art, P.S. 1 Museum, made a studio available in which the project was developed. Jessica Brackman, of FPG International, New York, was enthusiastic and supportive of our efforts, and this book could not have been done without her. Researchers and administrators at the following picture sources helped us, as well: Christine Argyrakis, Selma Brackman, Mary Jane Cannizzaro, Wendy Cope, Greg Schreck, Gary Elsner, Wendy Missan at FPG International; Roberta Groves of H. Armstrong Roberts; Tyrone Georgiou, Chairman, Art Department, SUNY, Buffalo; Bill Chychota, Ewing Galloway; Pierce Rafferty and Marion Fetas, Petrified Films, Inc.; Anne Grabitz, American Stock Photography; Eugene Ferrara, *The New York Daily News*. Phil Block, Director of Education at the International Center of Photography, Joel Sternfeld, photography department, Sarah Lawrence College, and Stephanie Hightower of The Cooper Union helped us find student interns who worked on the project; thanks also to Daniel Canogar, Janiel Englestadt, Lisa Rosen, Kara Walker and Sara O'Donnell.

Special thanks to David Corey, Susan Jonas, Dennis Kardon, Susan Kismaric, Charles Lahti, and the New York Department of Sanitation, who helped in the search for the transparencies in this book when they were stolen. Our gratitude to Lai Ng, the manager of a Roy Rogers restaurant, who not only found the material but returned it to us.

PHOTO CREDITS

Front cover, p. 5, 10, 22, 38, 56–57 (center), back cover: © Dennis Hallinan, FPG International Corporation; p. 1, 3, 13, (center), 23, 24–25, 26 (left), 32, 35, 89 (top left), 89 (bottom right): American Stock Photography; p. 2: Karsh, Ottawa Woodfin Camp and Associates; p. 4, 12, 20 (bottom right), 46, 58, 76, 91: Ewing Galloway, Inc.; p. 6–7: © Alpha, FPG; p. (top right), 19, 27, 31: Petrified Films; p. 8, 28, 30, 47, 62–63: © Laszlo Willinger, FPG; p. 9, 52, 60, 61, 65, 66, 67, 70–(center), 80, 83, 88, 92: H. Armstrong Roberts, Inc.; p. 11: © J. M., FPG; p. 12 (bottom right), 20, 21 (bottom right), 7 Reorganized Church of Jesus Christ of Later Day Saints/Buffalo Archive at Suny–Buffalo Art Department; p. 14–15: FP p. 16: © Beattie, FPG; p. 17: Robert Edgar; p. 18: © Burton Berinsky, 1989; p. 21, 54: © Stan Sholik, FPG; p. 26 (right © Rudy Miller, FPG; p. 29: © A. McCoy, FPG; p. 33: Niel Frankel; p. 34: © Jay Brenne, FPG; p. 34 (bottom cente Courtesy National Aeronautics and Space Administration, Washington, D.C.; p. 36–37: © F. Wilson, FPG; p. 39: Ire Vandermolen, © FPG; p. 39 (center): Photofest; p. 40, 45, 53: © Margerin Studio, FPG; p. 41: Burk Uzzle; p. 42 (left), 42– (center): Frederick Lewis, Inc.; p. 43 (right): © William Cramp, FPG; p. 44: Charles Harbutt/Actuality; p. 48: © Micha Simpson, FPG; p. 49: © Nancy McFarland, FPG; p. 50: © Robert Rathe, FPG; p. 51, 77, 78, 84–85: © Michael A. Kell FPG; p. 55: © L. Grant, FPG; p. 56 (left): © Zimmerman, FPG; p. 57 (right): © D. Spindel, FPG; p. 59: The Nation Archives, Washington D.C.; p. 62 (bottom left): Jimmy Carter Library; p. 64: © Steven Gottlieb, FPG; p. 68: © A. Upit FPG; p. 69: © J. Sylvester, FPG; p. 70–71, 81: © Pictor International, FPG; p. 72: After Image/Frank Fisher 1989; p. 7 Jack Knightlinger, Official White House Photographer; p. 75: © Jeffrey W. Myers, FPG; p. 75 (center): © John T. Turn FPG; p. 79: © E. A. McGee, FPG; p. 82: © John Farrell, FPG; p. 85 (top right): David Valdez, The White House; p. 8 © Henry Gris, FPG; p. 87: After Image/Gabe Palmer 1989; p. 90: © K. Kursh, FPG; p. 93: © Harry Bleyenberg, FP p. 95: © Jim Howard, FPG.

Excerpt on page 89 is from *The Complete Works of Aristotle: The Revised Oxford Translation*, edited by Jonathan Barne Bollingen Series 71. Copyright © 1984 by Jowett Copyright Trustees. Published by Princeton University Press.

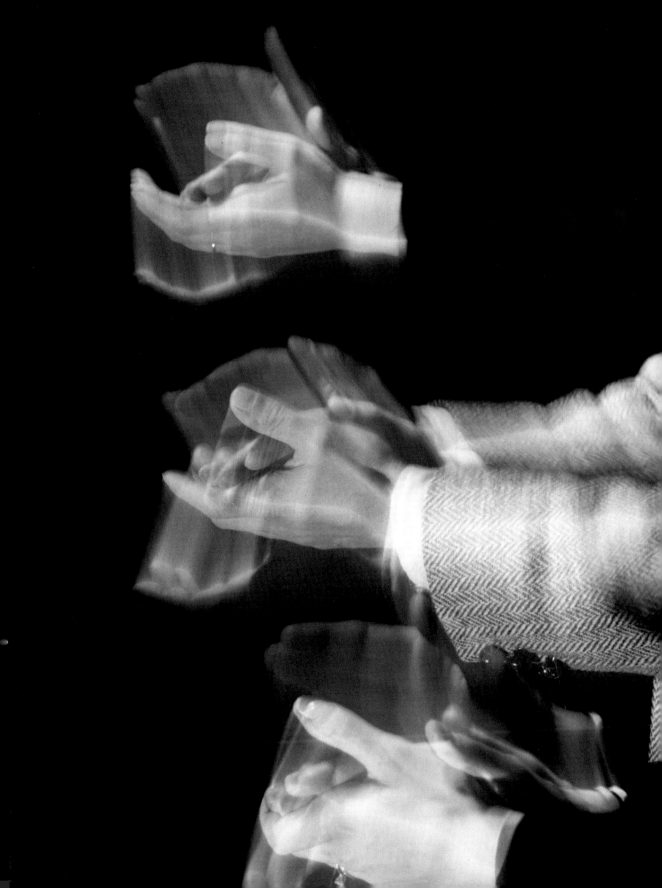

A VINTAGE ORIGINAL, JANUARY 1990
FIRST EDITION

LIBRARY OF CONGRESS CATALOGING-IN-PUBLICATION DATA
Heiferman, Marvin.
I'm so happy/Marvin Heiferman, Carole Kismaric.—1st ed.
p.   cm.
"A Vintage original"–T.p. verso.
ISBN 0-679-72095-2 : $10.95
1. Happiness–Pictorial works. 2. Photography–Portraits.
I. Kismaric, Carole, 1942–   . II. Title.
BF575.H27H45   1989
779–dc20   89–40124
                                                   CIP

Manufactured in the United States of America
10 9 8 7 6 5 4 3 2 1